CLOWNS

by
Harriet Langsam Sobol
photographs by
Patricia Agre

Coward McCann & Geoghegan, Inc.
New York

People in the Photos

"Gino" of the Cumeezis, N.Y.C.'s resident clown troupe: *p.5* The Cumeezis, N.Y.C.'s resident clown troupe: *p.6* The Cumeezis, N.Y.C.'s resident clown troupe: *p. 6* John Towsen: *p.7* "Bananas" of the Cumeezis: *p.8* John Towsen: *p.9* John Towsen as "Blondini": *p.10* David Kasakove of the Cumeezis becoming "Pish": *p.10* Raymond Clark of the Clyde Beatty—Cole Brothers Circus: *p.11* Gary Henry of the Hoxie Brothers Circus: *p.12* Sandy Kozik of the Clyde Beatty—Cole Brothers Circus: *p. 13* Mark Friesen of the Clyde Beatty—Cole Brothers Circus: *p.14* The Cumeezis, N.Y.C.'s resident clown troupe: *p.14* Sandy Kozik of the Clyde Beatty—Cole Brothers Circus: *p.15* Jonathan Kligler: *p.16* Jonathan Kligler: *p.16* Jonathan Kligler with children: *p.17* Mark Friesen of the Clyde Beatty—Cole Brothers Circus: *p.18* Glenn DeSantis with "Eggs" and "Pish" of the Cumeezis: *p.19* Kenny "Gumby" Columbo and Robert "BoBo" Mennillo: *p.20* The Cumeezis, N.Y.C.'s resident clown troupe: *p.21* Kenny "Gumby" Columbo and Robert "BoBo" Mennillo: *p.21* Clown Alley, Clyde Beatty—Cole Brothers Circus: *p.21* Charles "Chuckles" Crespo of the Clyde Beatty—Cole Brothers Circus: *p.22* Gary Henry of the Hoxie Brothers Circus: *p.22* Raymond Clark of the Clyde Beatty—Cole Brothers Circus: *p.23* Judith Landis of the Cumeezis becoming "Bananas": *p.23* Gary Henry of the Hoxie Brothers Circus: *p.24* Clowns of the Clyde Beatty—Cole Brothers Circus: *p.24* Fred Yockers as "Fritz": *p.25* John Towsen as "Blondini": *p.26* Fred Yockers as "Fritz": *p.27* Fred Yockers as "Fritz": *p.28* Richard Davidson of the Seattle Mime Theater: *p.29* John Towsen as "Blondini" and Fred Yockers as "Fritz": *p.30* John Towsen as "Blondini": *p.31* "Jasper" of the Cumeezis: *p.32*

ACKNOWLEDGMENTS

Special thanks to Jonathan Kligler, John Towsen and Fred Yockers. Thanks also to Mike Snider, John Kane, Gary Cavello, Sandy Kozik, Charles Crespo, Miguel Padille, Mark Friesen, Raymond Clark of the Clyde Beatty—Cole Brothers Circus; Gary Henry, of the Hoxie Brothers Circus; Eric Trules, Director, David Kasakove, Judith Landis, Mark Hellermann, Peg Evans, Caroline Ryburn, Peggy Florin, Peter S. Smith, of the Cumeezis; Robert Mennillo and Kenny Columbo; Glenn DeSantis; Ben Foose, Kristie Lambert, Marcus DiBernardo, Brian Lowrey, Rhonda Neal; James W. Raab; Jimmy James; Clyde Beatty—Cole Brothers Circus; Hoxie Brothers Circus; the Cumeezis, New York's resident clown troupe; and Nancy Krimm.

Library of Congress Cataloging in Publication Data
Sobol, Harriet Langsam. Clowns.
Summary: Follows the activities of clowns as they
dance, juggle, skate, put on costumes and makeup, look
silly or sad, and exercise their special magic.
1. Clowns—Juvenile literature. [1. Clowns]
I. Agre, Patricia, ill. II. Title.
GV1828.S59   791.3'3   82-1515
ISBN 0-698-20558-8   AACR2

To the clown in each of us

Let's follow the clown.
Come, join the parade.
The clown has a secret
but perhaps he will tell.

The clown works and practices
his dance and his tricks.

He stretches, he reaches,

he juggles,

he skates.

He walks on the rope.
He balances so well.

The clown is an actor
but he's something else,

something more.

He's a baggy-suit tramp,

a graceful whiteface,

or a bumbling fool.

His dress is quite splendid.
It glitters and shines.

But for some,
a hat is enough
or a very sad look.

He spends time with some children.
Does he tell them his secret?

**The clown does his tricks
at the circus,**

in the park,

or on a school stage.

The makeup is special.

Each face is his own.

Come on, hurry up!
It's time for the show.

Are you ready for the secret?
He's whispering it now.

He says he has magic ...
he knows how we feel

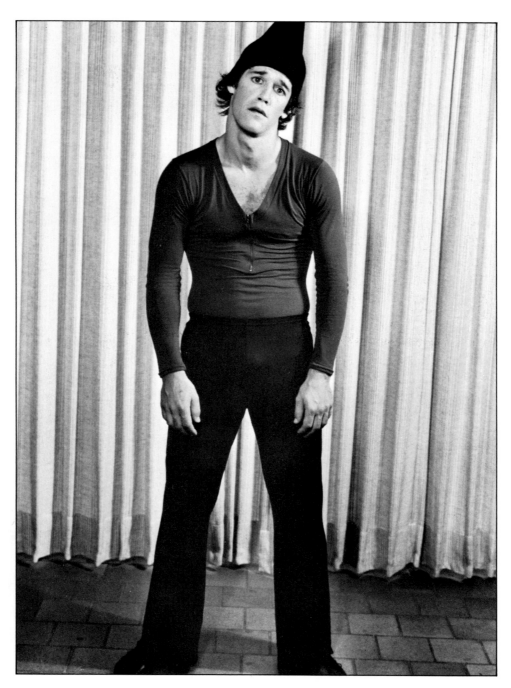

when we're silly or sad.

So we laugh at ourselves

when we laugh at the clown.